American Chestnut Tree Conservation Field Course

Manual for forest ecology and conservation of the North-East United States

First Edition

MARIYA CHECHINA, TOM SHOTZBARGER,

JOSEPH A. RESCH, YANNICK NEVEUX, OLGA SHER

© 2020 Antinanco Earth Arts School

Mariya Chechina, Tom Shotzbarger, Joseph A. Resch, Yannick Neveux, Olga Sher

Cover Illustration by Mark A. Klingler

Cover Design by Maxwell Shekoff

Grateful acknowledgement is made to Ayla Nereo, for permission to reprint an excerpt from her song "Whispers."

ISBN: 978-0-578-80693-8

A portion of proceeds from the sale of this book will go to support the Bring Back the American Chestnut Tree Project, an effort by Antinanco Earth Arts School to bring back the critically endangered American Chestnut Tree back to the North American forests.

Antinanco Earth Arts School is a non-profit community organization committed to preserving traditional and indigenous knowledge through environmental projects, education about the Earth, its inhabitants and ecosystems, and direct support of indigenous communities.

Holmdel, NJ 07733

Email: info@antinanco.org

www.antinanco.org

PREFACE

This manual is dedicated to the American chestnut tree, which was one of the most important wildlife-supporting trees in the United States. Squirrels, wild turkey, white-tailed deer, black bear, raccoon, passenger pigeon, Allegheny woodrat, and grouse depended on this legendary tree for their food and survival. Several unique insect species that relied upon chestnut trees as their principal food source became extinct. Once, the American chestnut tree covered over 200 million acres of eastern woodlands from Maine to Florida, and from the Piedmont plateau west to the Ohio Valley. Known as the "Redwood of the East," it often reached heights of 150 feet. Sadly, in the first half of the 20th century, 1 out of 4 trees across the range of eastern forests vanished because of an accidentally introduced disease, the chestnut blight. This is because across its range, the American chestnut comprised 25% or more of the forests' composition. Although the tree still exists today, it rarely has an opportunity to grow past sapling size or produce nuts. This manual is a part of the bigger "Bring Back the American Chestnut Tree" effort to restore the American chestnut tree to the Eastern Woodlands and discover ways to improve its health and growth.

DEDICATION

TO TREES:

To receive your whispers
tender breath-keepers
givers of life to these lungs
may I open my ears and surrender
what can you tell me
how can I tend you
how can I tend to the ones
who pour life through these lungs…

"We, for every one of us you've uprooted
you can soothe it by planting another
of the same as the kind you've uprooted
every ending a beginning if you choose it…
you can soothe it… if you choose it…"

'Whispers' by Ayla Nereo

Table of Contents

Course Summary and Purpose

This manual explores the topics of ecological principles to manage ecosystems. It teaches how to recognize forest disturbances (natural and introduced), recognize forest age, learn to identify dominant and understory species, learn the principles of basic tree identification, and measure biological diversity, tree growth and tree health. The manual specifically focuses on the conservation of the American chestnut tree species. The manual includes the American chestnut tree's ecological history and distribution, favorable soil conditions, companion plants and animals that depend on and disperse the chestnut, and major disturbances (natural and introduced) that impacted the chestnut distribution and caused the tree's ultimate disappearance.

The fieldwork component includes explanation on how to examine types of forest disturbances, identification of forest tree and non-tree species, measure soil pH and humidity, conduct forest transects, and how to collect, propagate and care for American chestnut seeds, seedlings and trees. The lab component includes information for labeling, pressing and examining leaves of different species under a microscope, making an identification key, recording field data and taking measurements with measuring tape, DBH tape and compass, calculating tree basal area and tree density, and testing soil pH. The manual teaches how to work with pH meters and pH strips, rope, compass, measuring tape, leaf press, and microscopes.

1.1 Background and Introduction to Forest Field Observations

1.1.1 Introduction

This section is designed to introduce students to forest field observation through learning how to identify basic forest features. This module focuses on techniques used to identify most common types of forest disturbance, regeneration strategy, and forest age or succession. Recognizing the main type of forest disturbance is key in understanding the main regeneration tactic. **Disturbance** is an integral part of forest development and change to the structure and composition of the ecosystem. It also allows for nutrients to be released. A **forest disturbance** is defined as an external event that causes partial or complete destruction of forest biomass. While these events are often seen as catastrophic in nature, they are actually an integral part of a forest ecosystem. In fact, forests and their species are usually adapted to the type of disturbance that is most common in the area, and these disturbances dictate forest regeneration strategy and 'successional dynamics.'

Successional dynamics refers to the stages of forest growth and maturity. **Early successional** species are colonizing species that can invade a cleared area or smaller gap formed after a disturbance. On the other hand, **mid and late successional species** can tolerate moderate to full shade and their seedlings can grow under a canopy of colonizing species. Forest disturbance intensity and frequency dictates forest composition, structure and function. For example, frequent but low intensity disturbance events tend to lead to many small gaps forming in the forest that will get invaded by fast growing early successional species. As a result of these gaps that form in mature forests, the overall forest biodiversity will be high due to early, mid and late successional species being present at the same time.

Large-scale events create a different dynamic that leads to **stand replacement.** This results in forest stands that are younger and are more uniform in age and species composition. These disturbances can be natural such as fires, landslides resulting from heavy rains or floods, wind (tornadoes, hurricanes and typhoons), volcanic eruptions, earthquakes, natural pathogens, and natural animal grazing. Human-caused disturbance (anthropogenic disturbance) is becoming more and more common and can be a lot more destructive. Anthropogenic disturbance includes climate change, pollution, logging, clearcutting, and the introduction of invasive species and pathogens. Here we will discuss disturbances related to the Northeast United States, and specifically, disturbances affecting the American chestnut tree.

1.1.2 Natural and Introduced Forest Disturbances and How to Recognize Them

The most common types of **natural forest disturbances** are **fire** (affecting Western US), **flooding** (affecting Eastern US) and **wind** (affecting Eastern US). **Fire disturbance** is common in boreal forests. It can range in frequencies from every 20 to 500 years. The intensity of the fire can also range from impacting the understory, ground level, or to complete stand destruction which range from small scale to landscape scale. The intensity and scale of the fires are directly impacted by what species are found in the forest. For example, there are several species that are known as fire embracing, such as the spruce (*Picea*). These species are highly flammable because they have needles with high resin content that easily catch on fire as well as low level branches that propagate ground fire to go up. These species also have cones that open and release seeds post-fire, so they use fires as a mode to propagate. Forests that have high quantities of spruce tend to have stand replacing fires. Conversely forests that have more larch (*Larix*) and pine (*Pinus*) species, which have higher moisture content, will have lower level ground fires. Ground fires are important in nutrient cycling as the fires burn the dry forest litter and release nutrients into the ground for the plants to use.

Flooding disturbance is common in lowland, floodplain forests. The periodic flooding recycles nutrients and sediments creating very rich soils as well as good environment for insects and birds. Trees such as the red maple, black ash, river birch and ironwood grow in these floodplain environments. These areas provide corridors for wetland species during the flood times and create breeding grounds for amphibians and insects. The floodplain ecosystems are very susceptible to **invasive plants** because of the rich soils as well as human encroachment. As a result, the biodiversity can be very high in these natural systems.

Wind disturbance is the most common type of disturbance that impacts the distribution where the American chestnut was found in rocky mountainous areas. Wind disturbance happens in areas that are prone to storms, hurricanes, typhoons. The disturbance varies by strength and frequency. Low intensity wind facilitates exchange of carbon dioxide and oxygen into the canopy and sub-canopy layer. Medium intensity winds that cause bending of the trunks and branch break offs cause the trees to invest photosynthate (products of photosynthesis) into structural reinforcement creating a thicker outer trunk layer. High-level intensity wind events can take out many smaller trees and can even damage the whole forest stand. High-intensity wind events are able to create gaps for early successional species recruitment increasing biodiversity. It can also create complete stand replacement where early successional species can invade the area and start the forest succession anew.

Pathogens are also a natural type of disturbance that can take out several trees, several species or even eradicate an entire patch when they attack a major keystone forest species. Pathogens can attack the roots, or cause cankers on the trunk and branches, or cause wilting of the leaves. They can also attack trees of various age. The most damage is done when pathogens attack recruiting young trees (recruiting is the process of young tree seedlings establishing into adults) before they have a chance to reproduce. Pathogens can cause serious damage to the tree's ability to uptake water and nutrients, weaken the trunk and branches, and damage the photosynthetic ability of the leaves. The pathogens can be bacterial or viral, and as long as they are not introduced (by humans and animals) or are invasive, trees usually learn how to evolve to withstand them. In a natural setting, these pathogens only affect the weakest individuals, reinforce natural selection, help maintain balance among tree species which decreases the ability of one species to dominate, and increase biodiversity. The spread of pathogens is becoming a bigger problem with increasing climate change and human activity.

Natural animal grazing is done mostly by deer and elk species in North America. When the density of these animals is relatively low, the damage to forest patches is not severe. However, grazing tends to destroy young recruiting trees which damages the reproduction of these species. Grazing damage can be more severe with domesticated animals that come in large herds. This is manmade, or anthropogenic disturbance.

Anthropogenic disturbance is becoming more and more severe due to increasing impacts of climate change, land clearing for human use, and forest extraction. **Climate change** is changing suitable conditions of many forest species, forcing them to limit their range to further north or upland, and creating situations where some will soon have no place to be. Climate change is also creating favorable conditions for invasive species and pathogens that cause devastation to forest stands as natural forests do not have mechanisms to combat invasive species. **Land clearing** for human use, such as building towns, parking lots, or malls is one of the most destructive forms of anthropogenic disturbances as permanent land use change prevents natural succession to return the area to vegetative states. **Clear cutting,** a method of forest extraction, can lead to large forest gaps, fragmented forest patches that limit natural recruitment. On the other hand, selective logging is not as damaging to the forest stand. But it can remove entire species due to logging preference, affect a larger area in order to collect the same amount of wood and thus create more roads and fragmentation. Finally, all the anthropogenic disturbances exacerbate impacts by natural disturbance as they weaken ecosystem function. As a result, it is very important to identify and be able to recognize signs of natural and introduced disturbance when attempting to rehabilitate a forest ecosystem.

1.1.3 Recognize Forest Age by Examining Forest Succession

Forest succession is a process of how forest tree species recover and regrow after a disturbance, or how these species colonize. **Early successional tree species** are fast-growing and sun-loving; they quickly create vegetative cover on degraded land and do not require fertile soils. Usually, their leaves, bark or roots have antibacterial or anti-fungal properties that deter pathogens, and this is used medicinally in many traditional cultures. However, these species will have poor survival and growth under an established tree canopy in a mature forest as they are intolerant of shade. Early-successional trees usually have wind-dispersed seeds that are light and small in order to be carried long distances. The early successional tree species' wood is usually soft and suitable for furniture but not used for building. They are generally short-living (however they can also be long living and big), but are able to change the natural environment (creating shade, changing microclimate, increasing water retention, and increasing soil fertility among others) that attracts other forest species and wildlife.

Mid successional species are secondary colonizers. They require semi-shade to thrive and invade areas that have already been colonized by early successional species. They have slower growth and are longer-living than early successional species. They help forests to transition from primary to secondary succession. They usually have fruits that are a bit larger in size than fruits of average early successional species. These fruits are dispersed in a wide variety of ways including wind, animals and birds that consume the fruit dispersing the seeds. These species in North America include red maple, black and yellow birch, white pine, white and red oaks, and hickories.

Late successional species are slow growing, shade-needing trees that colonize well established forest patches and lead to climax forest. Their seeds are large and heavy in most cases and are dispersed mostly by animals. Their wood is very dense and ideal for construction. They form the long-lasting structure of the forest canopy. Late successional species in North America include fir, spruce, hemlock, beech, chestnut, oak, sugar maple and yellow birch. Once the forest has reached climax with addition of late-successional species, it is still in the process of change through tree death, decomposition, gap creation through disturbance and invasion of early successional species.

American chestnut (*Castanea dentata*) is sun loving and fast growing tree that can also grow more slowly in shade. Its seeds are animal dispersed and it is a dominant, long living tree. What do you think of its successional strategy? We will discuss it in a later part of the manual.

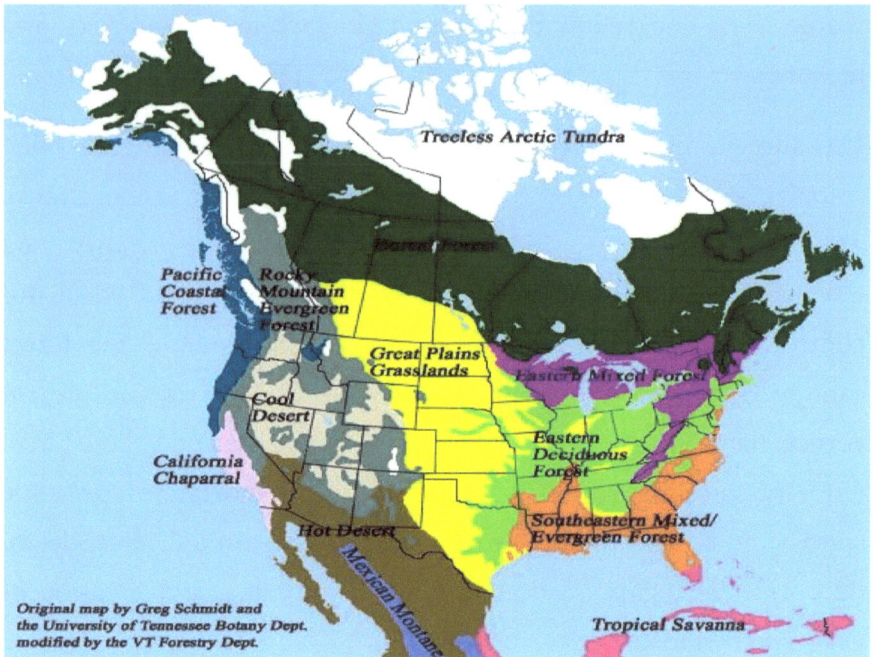

Figure 1.1 General Ecoregions of North America.

The ecoregion where the American chestnut tree used to be common is the Eastern Mixed Forest and the Eastern Deciduous Forest ecoregions. They can still be found there, but the trees are extremely sparse and they rarely reach mature size. The dominant broadleaf trees in this biome at its climax include oaks (*Quercus* spp.), beeches (*Fagus* spp.), maples (*Acer* spp.), or birches (*Betula* spp.). Finding large individuals of these species in a forest patch is a good indication that you are in a late-successional forest. Mixed forest also may include coniferous species such as pines (*Pinus* spp.), firs (*Abies* spp.), and spruces (*Picea* spp.).

1.2 Fieldwork

Based on the concepts that we have learned in previous sections on forest succession and disturbance, we will discuss how to recognize these features in a forest patch. It's important to be able to recognize forest disturbance and approximate forest age for anyone interested in forest conservation, reforestation or forest management.

1.2.1 Signs of Forest Disturbance: Type, Frequency, Severity

In this section, we will discuss how to identify disturbance most commonly encountered in Eastern North America and in the range of American chestnut trees. In order to determine what disturbances occurred in a forest patch, it may be important to speak with someone who knows the natural history of the area. If that is not an option, some observation may be able to tell you what had occurred. These observations should be done in the center of the forest patch. Start by marking off an area within your area of view and record observations of overall spacing of trees (dense or sparse), overall age, number of forest levels or strata, number of species in each strata, signs of fire and cut trees. Forest strata can be divided into understory trees or the young tree recruits with thin stems measuring 0.5 to 2 inches, suppressed trees or trees between 2 and 5 inches in diameter with crowns under a canopy of larger trees, dominant trees that are over 5 inches in diameter and have crowns at the top layer of forest canopy exposed to the sun, emergent trees are large trees well above 5 inches in diameter with crowns above forest canopy (see Figure 1.7)

We should be able to identify the severity, type and frequency of disturbance. If we are in a forest stand that is uniform in age, we can assume that this forest periodically experienced high intensity disturbance. High intensity disturbance destroys all standing trees and new trees that regrow have the same starting point, forming uniform age stands. On the other hand, a forest that looks diverse with many different species of various ages, likely experiences low intensity disturbance. Look for signs of understory, note any old large trees, and make observations of dead trees. Looking at dead trees can give you a clue about the type of disturbance. For example, forest fires will leave visible fire damage to trees while wind disturbance will have fallen trees that are cracked at the stem. See Figure 1.2 for examples of low intensity and high intensity fire occurrence in a forest stand.

Figure 1.2. Example of low intensity ground level fire-causing superficial damage to established trees and total damage to young trees (left) and stand level fire disturbance (right)

If the fire occurred over 10 years ago, the forest would have recovered with few visible damages to trees and a core sample may need to be taken to see if fire is in the history of any are trees (see description of core sampling below on page 13). If fires are more recent (within past 10 years) you may still be able to see the signs of fire on standing trees in the form of scars and overgrown uneven bark. It is beneficial to identify the species of the tree that has a scar as some species tend to be more prone to fire.

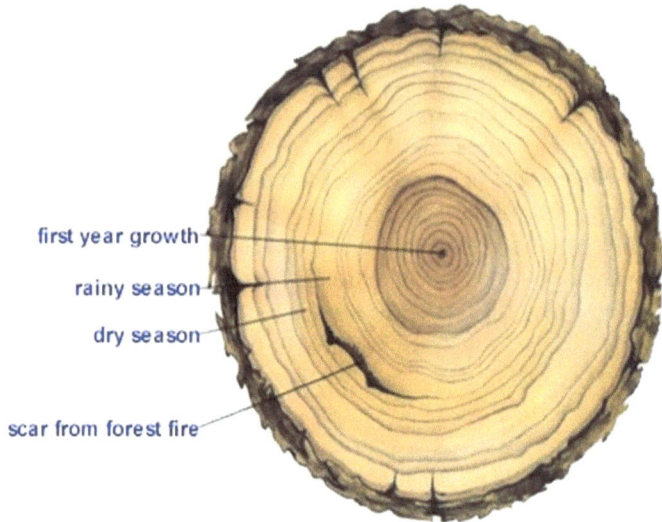

first year growth

rainy season

dry season

scar from forest fire

Figure 1.3. Tree rings seen on a cross section of a tree showing rainy and dry season growth, fire scars and tree age (each ring represents a year of growth).

For example, trees that have resin are a lot more flammable such as lodge pole pine. In fact, fire inducing species often need fire to release their seeds. If the patch that we are observing has many trees of Lodge pole and Jack pine or Douglas fir, we can expect frequent fires to occur there. If we take a core sample or a cross section, we can count the rings between fire events to get an idea of their frequency. If you look at Figure 1.3, we will see that the tree cross section shows two events of fire happening 4 years apart. We can also see that the successive burns are on the same side likely because of wind and fire patterns that happen in the same direction. In addition to possible fire damage, a tree's cross-section can also tell you its entire life history, including the growth during dry and rainy seasons as well as winter and summer growth

Wind damaged stands will have many fallen trees either broken or uprooted (see Figure 1.4). The wind can sway and pull, destabilizing the roots. Tall trees with large crowns will be more impacted by strong winds. There is also a difference in how species are impacted by wind. Deciduous trees are more impacted by wind during the growing season when the leaves are out. Some species handle wind better such as sycamore (Platanus occidentalis), yellow poplar (Liriodendron tulipifera), and sweetgum (Liquidambar styraciflua), while black locust (Robinia pseudoacacia) have leaves that cluster and don't create a lot of drag. Stronger events may create larger gaps of fallen trees of all sizes. Large intense events will have uniform stands, but this is more uncommon with wind.

Figure 1.4. Forest patch showing fallen young trees and cracked stems.

We can also look for signs of pathogens. These signs may be found on the bark or leaves. Standing dead trees present a good case study for pathogen examination. For example, signs of chestnut blight on the American chestnut tree, or Emerald Ash Borer damage on the Ash tree can be found by examining the tree's bark (Figure 1.5). Look for any signs that may give you indication of damage by virus, bacteria or insects such as damaged bark, drying or eaten leaves, and insects living in trees. Also, presence of woodpeckers and dead leaves/branches on an apparently healthy tree can be an indication of parasites. Look for signs of animal grazing such as chewed branches/leaves on small trees.

Figure 1.5. Example of chestnut blight (left) and Emerald Ash Borer damage (right)

Additionally, look for signs of anthropogenic disturbance such as logging tracks, hiking trails, and cut trees. This can give us a clue at what elements may prevent a forest patch reaching a mature state and the possibility of introducing pathogens and invasive species.

1.2.2 Forest Patch Succession, Approximate Stand Age and Tree Age

We can understand forest succession by observing the crown structure of the forest. A mature forest will have had time without major disturbance to develop a complex crown structure. We will see dominant tree species as emergent trees of the canopy. There will be new recruiting trees under the main canopy of different ages and heights as seen in Figure 1.7 that describes succession. We can note the crown structure by setting up a transect (Figure 1.6) about the length of the field of view (about 150 feet) and walking along it, noting all the different forest strata that is seen. Is there an understory? Are there many young trees under the canopy? Are there many large emergent trees? Presence of large trees will inform about the approximate age of the stand, but to know the exact stand age will require interviews with local people that may know the natural history of the area. You can also take a core sample of a live tree to know its history, or measure its diameter to approximate the age.

Figure 1.6. Setting up a forest transect by measuring a straight line of a specified distance through the forest along which observations are made.

Figure 1.7. General forest succession showing early, mid and late succession with understory, young recruiting trees, large emergent trees in a forest patch.

Although tree size vary by species it can give you a clue about stand age. You can do that by measuring a diameter at breast height -DBH (Figure 1.8). Use a tape to measure the circumference and then convert to diameter (Diameter=Circumference/pi) or use a special diameter tape designed to measure trees at breast height. You can then estimate tree age using an approximate growth factor noted for common species listed below. The formula to figure out the approximate age of particular species is Growth Factor x Diameter (in inches). For example, species that are fast growing will have a large diameter at an earlier age than mid or late successional species.

Figure 1.8. Measuring diameter at breast height of an old growth tree.

Table1.1: Tree species growth factor

Tree species	Growth Factor
American Chestnut	2.5
Red Maple	4.5
Silver Maple	3.0
Sugar Maple	5.0
River Birch	3.5
White Birch	5.0
Shagbark Hickory	7.5
Green Ash	4.0
Black Walnut	4.5
Black Cherry	5.0
Red Oak	4.0
White Oak	5.0
Pin Oak	3.0
Basswood	3.0
American Elm	4.0
Ironwood	7.0
Cottonwood	2.0
Redbud	7.0
Dogwood	7.0
Aspen	2.0

To take a trunk core sample for life history one can use a core borer. A core borer is a little invasive but not deadly to the tree. It screws into the trunk of a tree and one can then pull the core sample. The coring should be done at breast height and at the center of the trunk.

It is important to know the diameter of the tree to know if the borer is long enough. If the diameter is 20 inches we only need to core 10 inches, or half way in. The borer should be at least 10 inches long. The borer has three parts: the handle, the screw bit and the extractor. Assemble the borer by inserting the bit into the handle and insert in the tree. The core sample is taken by twisting the borer in. When you are all the way in, insert the extractor part, twist in the opposite direction a few times to release the core and then pull out the extractor which will release the core. Remove the borer by twisting it out of the tree. The sample can give us information about tree age, summer and winter growth patterns (summer growth is larger), as well as dry and wet years (wet years will have larger rings). We can also see fire scars on a core sample.

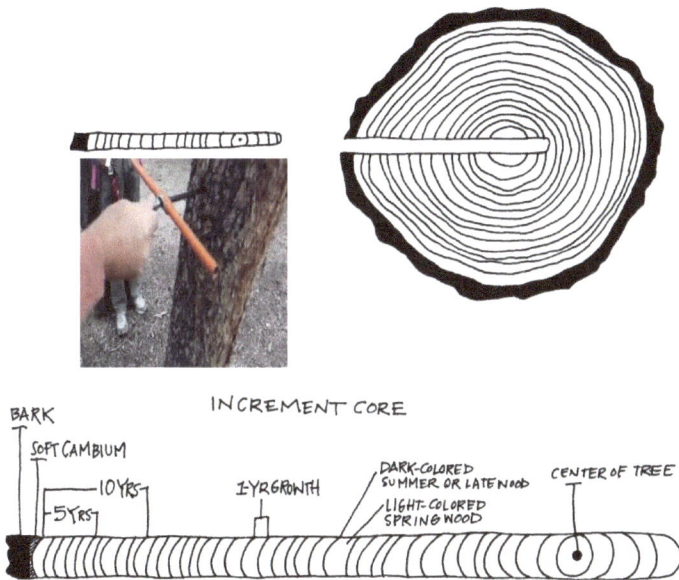

Figure 1.9. Using a core borer to take a core sample of a tree.

In order to identify tree age, stand age and biodiversity, it is important to be able to identify tree species. This can be simply done by looking at leaves, fruits, and bark of tree species. Use a tree guide for your area to be certain. Figure 1.10 shows leaves of common tree species in North America, but more precise guides are available for specific areas. You can note species and count biodiversity by setting up a transect line through the forest along which tree species are recorded. We will discuss biodiversity measures in the next section.

1.2.3 Basic Tree Identification

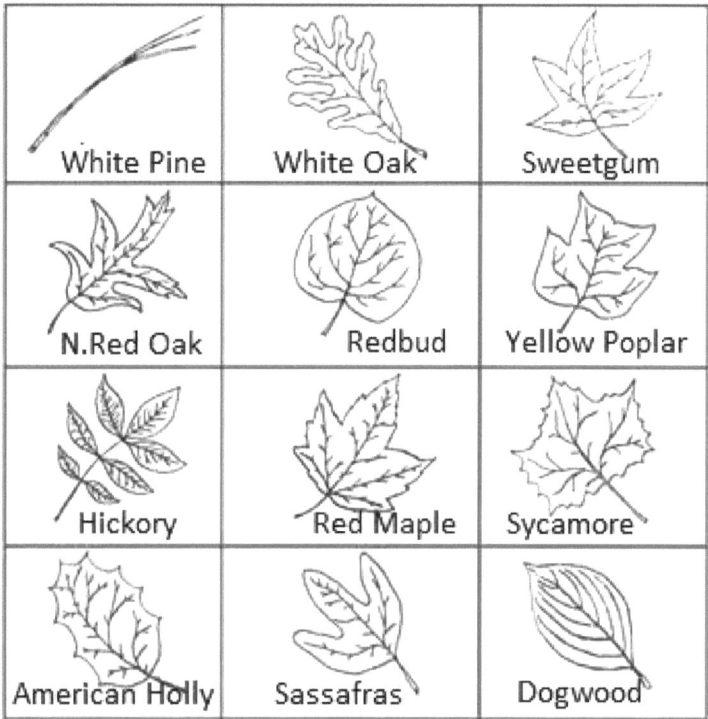

White Pine	White Oak	Sweetgum
N.Red Oak	Redbud	Yellow Poplar
Hickory	Red Maple	Sycamore
American Holly	Sassafras	Dogwood

Figure 1.10. Common trees found in North American forest stands.

In order to identify tree age, stand age and biodiversity, it is important to be able to identify tree species. This can be simply done by looking at leaves, fruits, and bark of tree species. Use a tree guide for your area to be certain. Figure 1.10 shows leaves of common tree species in North America, but more precise guides are available for specific areas. You can note species and count biodiversity by setting up a transect line through the forest along which tree species are recorded. We will discuss biodiversity measures in the next section.

1.2.4 Take Environmental Measurement

Measure soil pH and humidity as indicators of what species may grow in that environment. We can also look at general soil structure. Pedology, or soil study, can inform about soil fertility, composition and decomposition. The top layer can tell you about how much decomposition is happening (look for black organic matter), and thus how rich the soil is. The layer under the top layer can indicate drainage levels i.e. rocky/sandy (drain easily), clay (hard even for roots so doesn't drain thus could be swampy), mixed clay & organic matter (porous so can drain, but also retains some water), or in between sand and clay. We can also take note of soil texture coarseness, dryness and compactness, keeping in mind that wet and well aerated soils are best suited for forest trees.

Look for soil color to detect *lixiviation*, or percolation of soluble matter. Red or yellow color indicates the presence of iron oxides, thus signifying soil that is poor in humus and most minerals except for potassium. Red or yellow soils are generally acidic. Dark brown or black soils are usually rich in organic matter and are more fertile. Look at the amount of sloping as slope is an indication of drainage and soil richness. The bottom of the slope would have richer soils. We can also look at soil acidity using vinegar to see bubbling for basic pH, or baking soda to identify acidic soils. A simple pH test strip can identify the pH level. Most trees prefer to grow in neutral to only slightly acidic pH levels, while others such as American chestnut, prefer more strongly acidic soils. Finally, water is an important component of forest ecosystem. We can measure humidity with a hygrometer as an indication of moisture present in soils, even if humidity is measured in the air, as trees release water vapor during transpiration. Air humidity can tell us about tree density. In a dense forest, air humidity will likely be higher.

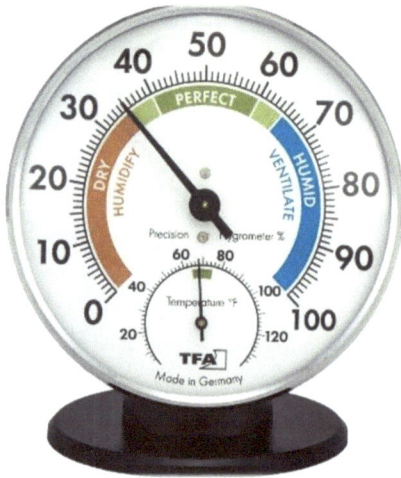

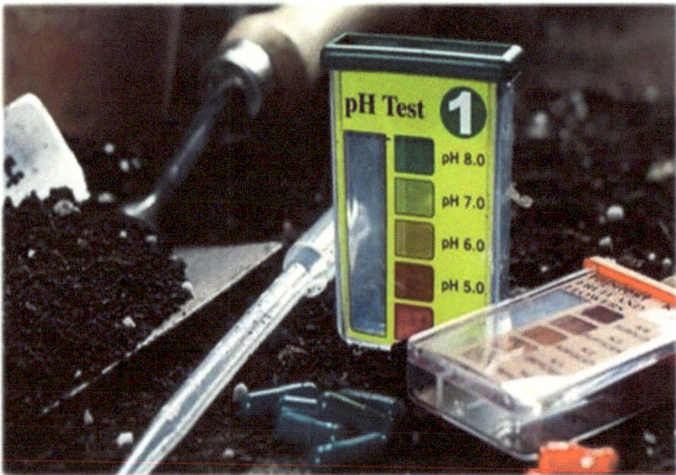

Figure 1.11. Hygrometer and a soil pH meter.

2.1 Forest Ecology Data Collection and Questions It Can Answer

Here we will go into more detail about forest biodiversity and forest health indicators, how to measure them by collecting data in the field and how to analyze and to summarize the data. This section will prepare students to plan and execute data collection for understanding animal and plant biodiversity in a forest patch and to determine forest health and relative age.

2.1.1 Biological diversity and what it can tell us about forest health

Biodiversity is the variety of plant and animal life on the planet or in a specific area. Biodiversity is also interchangeable with terms like species diversity or species richness. High biodiversity means there is a large variety of living things in an ecosystem. The reason why we want to see high biodiversity is because different forms of life provide different services to the ecosystem or occupy different niches within the ecosystem. For example, fruit trees provide food for animals, and in turn, these frugivores disperse the seeds of trees. Different species of mushrooms, or fungi help to decompose dead trees and return the nutrients back to the soil. Many insects depend on flowers for a food source and, in turn, pollinate these plants. There are abundant examples of these interactions, and in fact, animals and plants in a forest ecosystem are tightly interconnected.

In a high biodiversity system, many plants or animals can fulfill similar ecosystem services or occupy similar niches within an ecosystem. That is generally a good thing as it increases ecosystem resiliency. If only one species fulfills a specific ecosystem role, a sudden event that causes that species to disappear will reduce resiliency of the ecosystem through losing an important ecosystem function. For example, when the chestnut blight struck in the early 1900s, it wiped out 90% of all native chestnut trees in under 40 years. Many animals such as squirrels, bears, turkeys, deer and others depended on the chestnut for food, and experienced a decline in populations as a result of the American chestnut decline. As many as 60 different insect species relied on American chestnut. In particular, the American chestnut moth, which relied exclusively on the American chestnut became extinct. The reason why so many animal and plant species suffered as a result of sudden decline in American chestnut is because it was the main occupant of its niche and other sources of food for these animals were not as abundant or preferred. A highly resilient system would have a few species existing in similar abundance under conditions of healthy competition that can fulfill the same niche. If one of these species were to disappear, other species that occupy similar niche would take over and spread to fulfill the ecosystem service without much change to the overall ecosystem.

2.1.2 Why do we measure biodiversity

We measure biodiversity to gain a deeper understanding about an ecosystem. High biodiversity is usually associated with better ecosystem health and resilience. There are some nuances to this notion. First, biodiversity is usually higher in warmer climates, and it peaks at the equator due to a year-round growing season.

Biodiversity is lowest at the poles where it stays cold. On a smaller scale, biodiversity is highest in places near the edges of ecosystems, such as borders of forest patches. The edge tends to be more open allowing early successional species to invade the space. This results in an environment that is suitable to a mix of late, mid and early successional species and increases biodiversity. Ecosystems that are in transition or are still in early stages of succession may also show high biodiversity. On the other hand, stable climate forest ecosystems will most likely have lower biodiversity than early successional changing systems. It's important to understand these interactions because high biodiversity is not always an indication of good ecological health. For example, a highly fragmented ecosystem with many borders and edges between ecosystems would likely have higher biodiversity than a uniform climax forest. For that reason, we have to take into account the degree of fragmentation as well as other measures of forest ecosystem health.

2.1.3 How to measure biodiversity and what are some forest health measures?

Biodiversity can be measured in a few different ways based on what you are trying to understand about the ecosystem. For example, as we discussed already, fragmented landscapes may have a high number of individual species due to the presence of new colonizing species in addition to the established species on the undisturbed part of the ecosystems. On the other hand, an established undisturbed forest may have fewer individual species than a disturbed one but will have more balance between the numbers of each species. As a result, a good biodiversity measure will take into account species richness, or number of species present, and species evenness, which takes into account the number of individuals for each species. Sites with low species evenness might have high species richness, but it means that few species are very abundant and the species richness is due to many rare species.

Biodiversity measures also will change depending on scale. Small scale biodiversity is measured at a habitat unit, for example a forest patch, and is known as alpha diversity. Alpha diversity refers to species richness and focuses on identifying the number of different species in a small area. Beta diversity measures biodiversity between 2 habitats, for example an old growth forest patch and a young recruiting forest. Beta diversity is also diversity that is measured along a gradient such as forest species change going along an elevation gradient. Beta diversity is used to compare how an ecosystem changes going up the slope. Gamma diversity measures biodiversity within a landscape or a region. The gamma diversity also measures a rate at which new species are added to a landscape. Figure 3.1 gives an example of measuring biodiversity on different scales. Alpha diversity would measure biodiversity of 7 at site A, 5 at site B, and 7 for site C. Beta diversity would measure 11 species between site A and Site B since there is one species in common. Gamma diversity for the landscape would be 13 since there are many species common between the three sites.

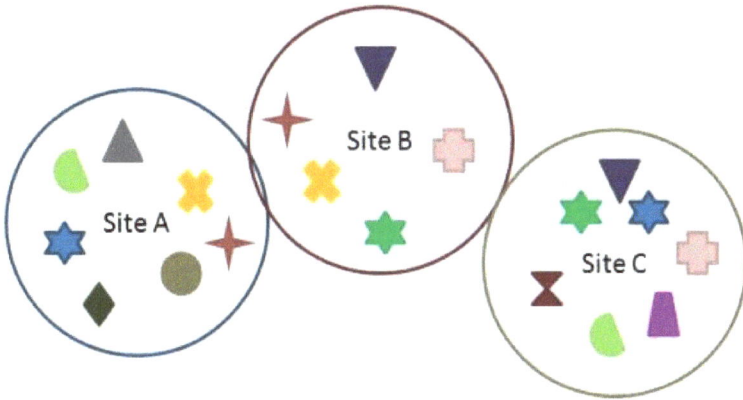

Figure 2.1 Diagram showing biodiversity at 3 different habitats where each unique symbol represents a different species.

2.2 Fieldwork

In this section we will go over what you will need to prepare, plan and collect data in the field. We will also discuss how to properly collect and record data, as well as how to calculate basic biodiversity and forest heath indicators.

2.2.1 Preparing data sheets for taking measurements in the field

Before going out in the field, it's important to make sure that you know what data to collect and to plan how you are going to do it. Some of the basic measurements that we can take in the field are recording different species of trees (or understory plants) that are there in a certain area. We may want to know how many of each species there are approximately. For each individual species, we may want to know the number of old versus young trees. To collect this information, we will make a data table and plan what data we will collect. To know the different species present, we can perform a simple transect data collection where all the different species of trees and other vegetation are noted along a selected line in the forest. But for quantitative measurements, we will select a representative area of the forest and mark off a square area where we will collect the measurements, our study area. In order to know the number of different species present, we will need to note the species name or the common name of all trees in our study area. We may need to use an identification key that lists common tree species for our area. We will then also record the X and Y location of each tree within the study area to know the distribution of the species in the study area. We will take the girth (diameter at breast height which is standardized to be taken at 4.5 feet from the ground, DBH) and height measurements of each tree to know the age distribution of trees in each species in our study area. Next, we will mark the crown position of the tree to know its successional status among its neighbors. As a result, our table for data collection will need to be like Table 2.1:

Table 2.1 Example of a data table for entering field data.

ID	Name	X location	Y location	DBH	Height	Crown position
1	C.dent					
2	Q.alba					
3	A.rubr					
4	P.stro					
5	P.occi					

In the column where we will record the name of the trees, we generally use a code to simplify note taking in the field. For example, we will use first letter of genus name followed by four first letters of species name. For American chestnut, the code is C.dent based on the scientific name *Castanea dentata*, White oak is Q.alba for *Quercus alba*, Red maple is A.rubr for *Acer rubrum*, White pine is P.stro for *Pinus strobus*), and Sycamore is P.occi for *Platanus occidentalis* .

The table also has columns for recording tree **ID**, **X and Y location** of each tree, **DBH** measurement for each tree, **height**, and **crown position**. All of the measurements, except crown position, are generally recorded either in meters/centimeters or feet/inches. We may also need to record the date of when the measurements are taken and who is doing the recording.

Crown position is a relative measure and is recorded by visual observation to note the approximate crown position of emergent trees (E), dominant tree (D), sub-dominant tree (SD), suppressed (S) and understory (U) (see Figure 2.2). Crown position can tell us more about the forest composition and what tree species are dominant in the forest.

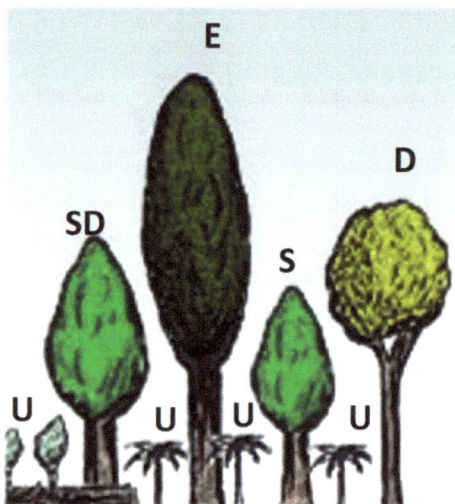

Figure 2.2. Crown position of a forest canopy. E is emergent forest strata, D is dominant forest strata, SD is sub-dominant forest strata, S is suppressed forest strata, and U is understory forest strata.

2.2.2 Establishing forest plots and transects for data collection

We already discussed briefly how to set up a **transect line**. Figure 1.6 shows an image of a field crew setting up a transect line. Generally, a transect is a straight line going through the study area along with the data to be collected, usually recording different animal or plant species present. A transect could be anywhere from 25 meters (75 feet) to 100 meters (300 feet) long, depend on your study area. If the study area is large and diverse, you will need a larger transect than in an area that is not diverse and small. You can start by picking a part of the forest that represents the general composition, on the interior of the forest. You will want to decide in which direction to make the transect line. If your transect goes from North to South direction, start at the North point and mark it off with a pole. From the North pole, measure out a half point going directly South using a long measuring tape (you can use a compass for precise measure) and put a pole. Then continue to mark the other half of the transect line. You can leave the tape measure in place or put a rope between the poles to mark off the area. Then start taking notes along the transect line and record all the species that you encounter right on the line. If the area is sparsely populated with tree, you may want to expend and record all trees 1, 3 or 5 feet in each direction from the transect line. The transect line is useful in assessing species that are present in the forest, or for comparing many different forest areas by setting up multiple transects in the forest.

For taking precise measurements on tree location, girth and height, you will have to set up a forest plot. To make it easiest, pick out a flat area within the interior of the forest that represents the forest ecosystem well. Set up a square plot within the flat area that was identified. Usually to get significant biodiversity measures, you will need to set up a one hectare plot (100 meters by 100 meters or 300 feet by 300 feet). A one hectare plot is the minimum to capture enough biodiversity that may represent the forest's total biodiversity. However, one hectare will take a long time to set up and measure. For the purpose of an exercise, we can start by setting up a 10 meter by 10 meter (30 feet by 30 feet) plot where all measures will be taken. You will need a compass, poles, rope and a measuring tape that is at least 10 meters (30 feet) long. Start by putting a pole in one corner and decide on the direction to go, let's say North-South (Figure 2.3). Pointing south from the pole, measure out 10 meters and put another pole. Now, do the same going east and then north. This will form the outline of a square. Now that you have all the poles set, you can tie the rope to mark off the study plot (see figure 2.4). You can now start taking measurements.

Figure 2.3 Setting up a forest plot or a transect line.

2.2.3 Taking measurements and recording data

It is important to know how to take each measurement for precise data collection. This manual will show you how to use simple tools to take all the measurements. Now that you set up the plot, you will be able to measure the X and Y location of each tree within the plot. You will start by identifying the X and the Y axis. The X axis is the South side of the plot that goes from West to East. The Y axis of the plot is the West side that goes North to South. To find the X location of a tree, you will start from the South West pole and start measuring with a measuring tape along the South side until you see the tree in question at a 90 degree angle (using a compass) from the X axis (the South side). The distance between the South West pole and where the tree is 90 degrees from the South side is the X location. To measure the Y location, start measuring from the North West pole and walk along the West side of the plot until you see the tree directly 90 degrees from the West side. The distance between the North West Pole and where the tree is 90 degrees from the side is the Y location (Figure 2.4).

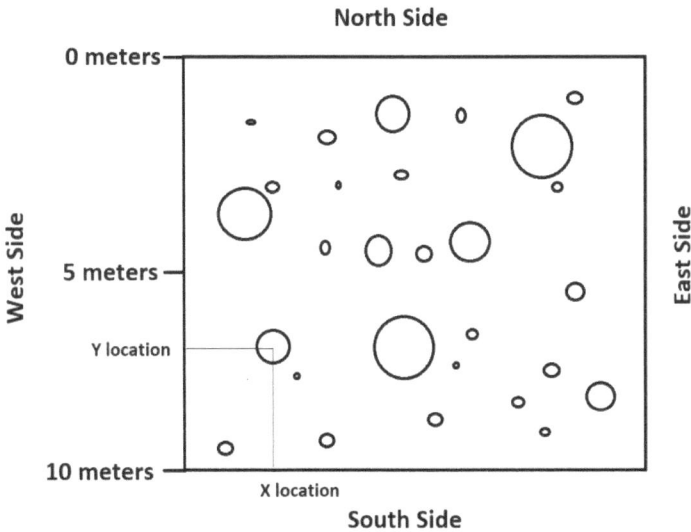

Figure 2.4. Study area showing individual trees (circles of different sizes) found within a study area of 10 meters by 10 meters. The figure also shows how to note the x and y locations of each tree.

Figure 2.5. Measuring the diameter at breast height of a tree with measuring tape.

Now let's measure the girth of the tree. You can measure the girth of trees that are at least 3 inches in circumference. For smaller trees, these measurements are difficult as they may not be yet of chest height. You can skip the measuring and just record the height instead, or record the base diameter, making a note that it was taken at the base. There are special DBH tapes that tell you the diameter of a tree when you measure around the tree. However, if you are using a regular measuring tape, what you will be measuring is the circumference. Wrap the measuring tape around the tree at the height of your chest (diameter at breast height) to make sure that you are measuring all trees at the same height. Tree trunks are slightly thicker all the way at the bottom and taper off to the top. So the measurements will be different depending where you take them. Diameter at breast height standardizes the measure and lets you compare tree girth because you take it at a standard height of 4.5 feet (Figure 2.5). If you use a standard measuring tape, you will need to convert circumference into diameter using the following formula:

$$Diameter = \frac{Circumference}{pi(3.14159)}$$

Now let's measure the tree height using some basic trigonometry.

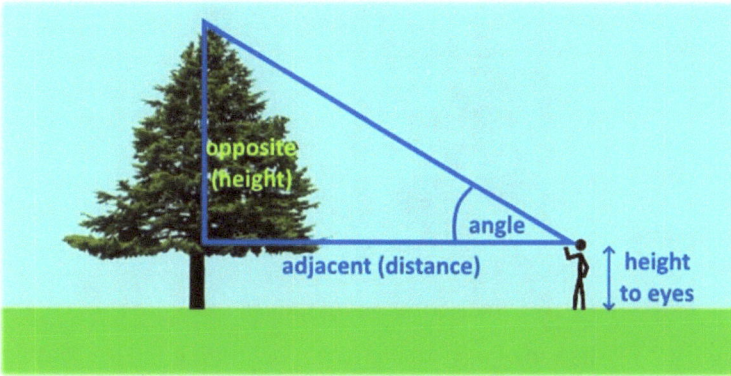

Figure 2.6 Method of measuring the tree height.

First, we have to move to a distance at which a crown of a tree that we want to measure can be seen and measure the angle as well as the distance (Figure 3.6). The height of a tree is:

$$Tree\ height = Height\ to\ eyes$$
$$+ tan(angle)\ X\ Adjacent(distance)$$

You can just record the measurements (distance and angle) in your notes and perform the calculations later. If you choose to do so, you may need to adjust the table to include angle and distance columns to replace the height column. Make sure you record the height of the person to their eyes and write it down somewhere on the data sheet to include in your calculations.

Figure 2.7. Method of measuring tree cover with a mirror that has gradations.

Let's now measure tree cover. These measurements will not go into the data sheet, but rather you can record it by drawing a map of the study plot dividing the plot area into sub-plots where tree cover is recorded (Figure 2.8).

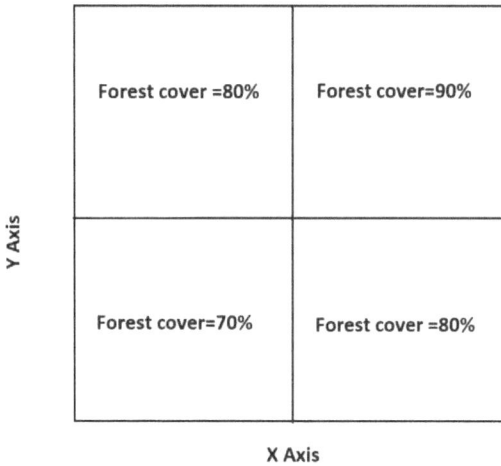

Figure 3.8. Map of the study area divided into 4 parts where forest cover is recorded in percent.

You may need to know what percent of the land is covered by forest to figure out how dense our forest is, and to know if we can find large wildlife. Large animals tend to prefer dense forest where they can hide from predators. Forest cover can also tell us more about the stage of forest succession. Mature forest will have thick forest cover besides having many large trees. Some compasses have a mirror in them with gradation. To measure the tree cover, stand in the middle of the sub-plot, point the mirror to the forest canopy and count the number of squares that have tree canopy. The sub-plots should not be more than 5 meters by 5 meters (15 feet by 15 feet). You can calculate percent cover by:

$$Percent\ forest\ cover = \frac{Number\ of\ occcupied\ squares}{Total\ number\ of\ squares} X\ 100$$

2.2.4 Calculating biodiversity and forest summary measures

From the measurements that we collected, we can now calculate several forest summary and biodiversity statistics. First, we can very simply calculate tree density since we know the area that we measured, and we know how many trees were measured. The density will be expressed as number of trees per meter (or foot):

$$Density = \frac{Number\ of\ trees}{Area\ (X\ distance * Y\ distance)}$$

We can also estimate the basal area, or the area that the trees occupy. To calculate it correctly, it helps to have the diameter at the base of a tree, but a DBH measure can closely estimate the area. The total basal area is the sum of each individual tree basal area, which is: $Area = pi * (diameter/2)^2$. As a result, the equation becomes:

$$Tota\ Basal\ area = \sum pi * \left(\frac{DBH}{2}\right)^2$$

We can calculate how much of the total plot area the trees occupy by converting the basal area to meters (meter=100cm) or feet (1 foot=12 inches), and dividing total basal area by total plot area, as long as they are in the same units.

We can also estimate tree volume now that we have the basal area and the height of the trees. For each tree, the formula to estimate the tree volume is to use a parabola volume formula that is thicker at the bottom and tapers off to the top and is given as:

$$Tree\ Volume\ (parabola) = 0.5 * Tree\ Basal\ Area * Height$$

Finally, we can also calculate biodiversity measures. The index we will use is the Simpson's index because it takes into account the species' richness and evenness. But to calculate it, we will need to summarize our data table by species. We do so by listing all different species found and count the number of individuals found for each species such as the example given below for 2 study plots:

Table 2.2 Number of individuals of each species found on pot 1 and plot 2.

Name	Number of individuals plot 1	Number of individuals plot 2
C.dent (American chestnut)	50	10
Q.alba (White oak)	20	150
A.rubr (Red maple)	30	5
P.stro (White pine)	75	15
P.occi (Sycamore)	25	20
Total	200	200

The formula to calculate the Simpson's index is the sum of the number of trees for each species divided by total number of trees squared:

$$Simpson's\ index = \sum \left(\frac{number\ of\ trees\ in\ a\ species}{total\ number\ of\ trees}\right)^2$$

The Simpson's index values range between 0 and 1, from 0 being infinite diversity and 1 being no diversity. We can calculate the index for 2 examples listed in table 3.2. They both have the same species, but plot 1 has a more even distribution of species than plot 2. The Simpson's index reflects that with a value of 0.25 for plot 1 and 0.58 for plot 2. Numbers closer to 0 signify higher diversity. As a result, because of better species distribution, plot 1 would have higher biodiversity than plot 2.

3.1 American Chestnut Management

This portion of the manual will discuss the American chestnut tree's natural distribution and ecological history, and why the tree is considered functionally extinct. This chapter will go into detail about the identifying features of the American chestnut and discuss its companion plants that help the species flourish.

3.1.1 American chestnut: natural history, distribution and disappearance

American chestnut (*Castanea dentata*) naturally occurred in the eastern North America, stretching from Southern Ontario and Maine, along the Appalachian mountain range to Mississippi, and from the Atlantic coast to the Ohio Valley (Figure 3.1). The American chestnut is a fast growing, long-living species that could once grow to be 60 to 80 feet tall or more and 5 to 10 feet in diameter, but generally reaches only a height of 40 feet or less at the present time. The American chestnut is a deciduous tree that is found in moderately moist (mesic) to dry (xeric) forests. It produces a large crop of edible nuts. Healthy trees start producing nuts at 7 to 10 years of age. The ability to produce a crop of edible nuts at a relatively young age is what used to help the species to spread and proliferate in its natural range.

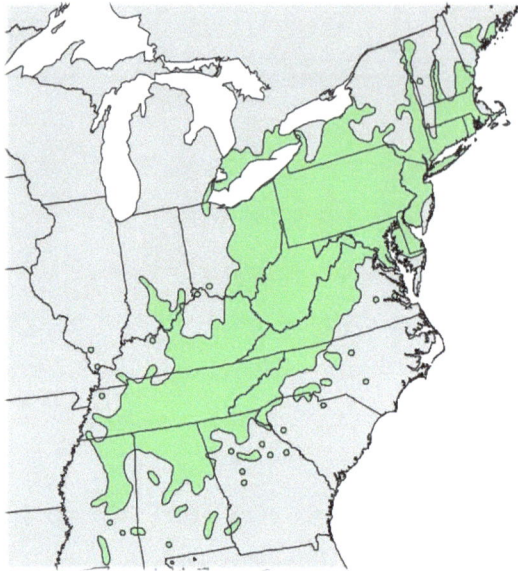

Figure 3.1 Natural range of the American chestnut (Castanea dentata)

In the 1800s, the tree's demise started with an ink disease (*Phytophthora cinnamomi*), which affected many trees in the southern range. Then in the early 1900s, the natural range of the American chestnut became accidentally infected by the chestnut blight (*Cryphonectria parasitica*) that entered the United States on chestnut trees (*Castanea crenata or Castanea mollissima*) imported from Asia. The chestnut blight is a parasitic fungus that attacks the inner bark layer of the tree causing shoot and trunk die-back. It usually enters a susceptible tree through a wound in the bark and causes a brown-red canker to form. The canker grows and spreads until it covers all around the bark of the trunk, causing that aboveground part of the tree to die. The disease can also infect other forest species such as the oaks, maples, and hickories, but does not cause death in these species. However, because of the pathogen's ability to persist in many different tree species, its eradication is nearly impossible. The chestnut blight was able to eradicate 98% of the standing chestnut trees in just over 40 years. The trees can sometimes re-sprout from the root of an infected tree, but will rarely reach maturity due to reinfection of the stem. As a result, most chestnut trees that exist today are only visible as small shrubs and young recruiting shoots, very rarely reaching reproduction.

Until the early 1900s, when the Chestnut blight was introduced and functionally eradicated the species, they were the dominant forest trees and occupied the ecosystem in great numbers. One in four trees throughout the species' range in the Appalachians was an American chestnut and it could occupy as much as 40% of the canopy. Many species of animals and plants depended on the American chestnut for food and shelter. The large crop volume provided food for white-tailed deer, wild turkey, passenger pigeon, black bears, many species of rodents. Species, like the American chestnut, that provide food and shelter for many animal and plant species are known as the **keystone species**. The keystone species usually define the ecosystem and the American chestnut did just that. Their loss to the chestnut blight made it that much more devastating as it altered the entire ecosystem that the American chestnuts were supporting.

The loss of the American chestnut tree resulted in a decrease in squirrel, deer, Cooper's hawk, cougar, and bobcat populations. The loss of the tree species also resulted in the extinction of 7 different moth species, and a drastic decline of many species of cavity nesting birds. The chestnut also provided good soil retention and water filtration ecosystem service. After the sudden loss of the chestnut tree, the water quality in nearby rivers and streams was affected, diminishing many fish and invertebrate populations. The dominant forest type in the Eastern US went from chestnut-oak to hickory–oak dominated forests. Hickory also produces a nut that is edible by wildlife. The tree helped to fill the niche, and several species of wildlife, like the deer and the squirrels slowly recovered. Later, the ecosystem further changed with the introduction of red maple that grows abundantly in the ecological range formerly occupied by the chestnut tree.

The American chestnut was also important economically. It had excellent timber properties suitable for construction. The trees usually grew straight and produced straight grain, light weight but durable and rot-resistant timber. One tree could fill an entire train car with boards. The wood was so versatile that it was used for construction, fine furniture making, and musical instruments. As a result of its properties, it was cultivated and sought after in the natural forest for timber and nut products. It made up a big part of the rural economy in the North Eastern US region. The nuts were used to feed livestock and for human consumption.

3.1.2 Identifying characteristics of the American chestnut

Identifying plant species is a great skill to have when conducting forest field assessment. Usually, the plants can be identified by looking at the leaves, bark, flowers and fruits. All types of chestnut trees have similar looking leaves, flowers and fruits with slight species specific difference. The chestnut tree is a deciduous tree with alternate leaves that are oblong, short-stemmed and veined. The leaves are fine-pointed and have large indentations with small bristles on the edges.

Table 3.1 Identifying characteristics of 10 most common chestnut species

	Common Name	Scientific Name	Identifying Characteristics
Group 1: 3 nuts per bur	American chestnut	*Castanea dentata*	Deeply indented, hairless leaves 5 to 10 inches long with sparse bristles on the bottom of the midrib; smooth red brown twigs; flowers at end of branches
	Dwarf Chinese chestnut	*Castanea seguinii*	Deeply indented, hairless (or almost hairless) leaves 2 to 4 inches long with glands on lower surface; twigs with short hairs; flowers at end of branches
	European chestnut	*Castanea sativa*	Hairy leaves on the lower surface 5 to 10 inches long; thick and coarse, brown smooth twigs; flowers at end of branches
	Chinese chestnut	*Castanea mollissima*	Leaves that have dense, hairs on the lower surface that are coarsely serrated and leathery; greenish-brown or buff-yellow twigs
	Japanese chestnut	*Castanea crenata*	Leaves that have dense or sparse hairs on the lower surface, bristle-like projections on leaves instead of teeth; dark reddish-brown downy twigs
Group 2: 1 nut per bur	Allegheny chinquapin	*Castanea pumila*	Leaves with dense hairs on lower surface, deeply indented margins and are 3 to 10 inches long; flowers on long spurs, small nuts
	Ozark chinquapin	*Castanea ozarkensis*	Leaves with dense hairs on lower surface, deeply indented margins and are 3 to 10 inches long, flowers on short side spur
	Florida chinquapin	*Castanea floridana*	Leaves with dense hairs on lower surface, deeply indented margins and are 3 to 10 inches long
	Trailing chinquapin	*Castanea alnifolia*	Leaves with dense hairs on lower surface, deeply indented margins and are 3 to 10 inches long
	Chinese chinquapin	*Castanea henryi*	Hairless leaves that have bristle-like teeth and are shaped like willow leaves, 3-6 inches long

Male flowers form on the stems in the form of long catkins that are as long as or longer than the leaves, while the female flowers form as shorter catkins. The nuts are formed inside prickly husks, called burs. The husks break open when the nuts have matured. There are many species of chestnuts that have slightly different identifying characteristics and the 10 most common ones are found above in Table 3.1:

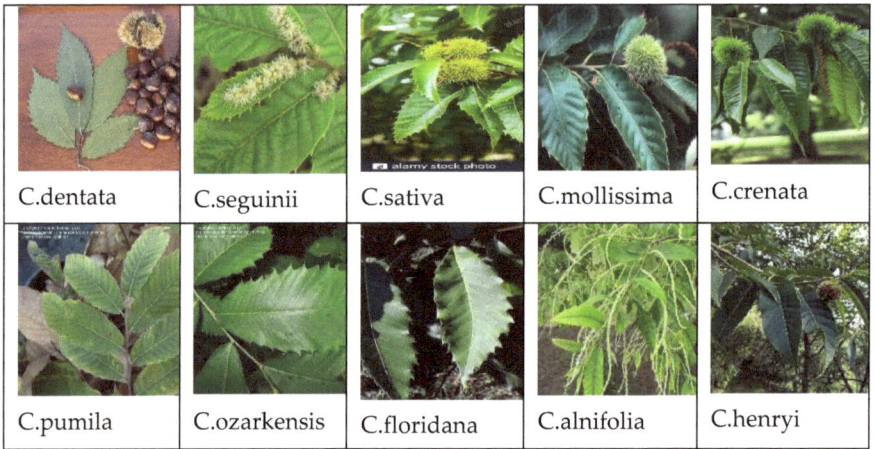

Figure 3.2. Images of 10 different species of chestnuts.

Figure 3.2 shows the leaves and fruits of 10 chestnut species corresponding to table 3.1. At first glance, these species look very similar. That is the reason why it is important to know and pay attention to several identifying features of the leaves, bark, flowers and/or fruits. Figure 3.3 shows the American chestnut catkins, burs and bark.

Figure 3.3 American chestnut catkins, nut burs and bark

3.1.3. Identifying characteristics of companion plants that grow well with chestnut

American chestnuts grew in their native habitat together with other native plants that provided beneficial nutrients and/or environment for the chestnut. Some of the common companions that we plant with chestnuts are shown in Figure 3.4 below, and identified by their common and scientific names. Plants that consume similar or same resources in the ecosystem and occupy the same niche are known as competing plants. On the other hand, plants that consume slightly different nutrients and occupy different niches, won't have to compete for these resources and can co-exist. In addition, many plants benefit from co-existing as they can contribute important exchange of nutrients to help each other. The companion plants do just that by interacting with the American chestnut via resource exchange. For example, the purple prairie clover and the slender bush clover are nitrogen fixing, which means that they can convert nitrogen gas into usable nitrogen in the soil, making it available for all plants, including the American chestnut. The American chestnut contained high amounts of potassium and other minerals in their leaves that also added nutrients back into the soil during leaf fall for the plants to use.

Other herbaceous flowering plants attract pollinators that the American chestnut also may have benefited from.

 Anise hyssop *Agastache foeniculum*	 Wild blue indigo *Baptisia australis*	 Purple prairie clover *Dalea purpurea*	 Tick-trefoil *Desmodium canescens*
 Slender bush-clover *Lespedeza virginica*	 Great blue lobelia *Lobelia siphilitica*	 Scarlet beebalm *Monarda didyma*	 Black-eyed Susan *Rudbeckia hirta*
 Wild Senna *Senna herbecarpa*	 Redbud *Cercis Canadensis*	 Honey locust *Gleditsia triacanthos*	 Black locust *Robinia pseudoacacia*

Figure 3.4 Identifying characteristics of 12 chestnut companion plants. The first 9 are herbaceous plants and the last 3 are nitrogen-fixing trees.

Red maple	Sassafras	Black & yellow	Shagbark hickory
Acer rubrum	*Sassafras albidum*	birch *Betula lenta*	*Carya ovata*
		&alleghaniensis	

Mockernut	White ash	Black ash	Tuliptree
hickory	*Fraxinus americana*	*Fraxinus nigra*	*Liriodendron*
Carya tomentosa			*tulipifera*

Chestnut oak	Northern red oak	White oak	Eastern white
Quercus montana	*Quercus rubra*	*Quercus alba*	pine
			Pinus strobus

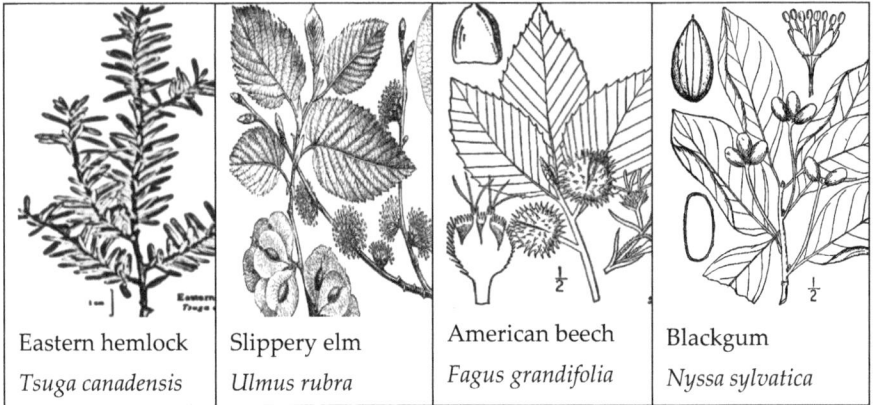

Eastern hemlock	Slippery elm	American beech	Blackgum
Tsuga canadensis	*Ulmus rubra*	*Fagus grandifolia*	*Nyssa sylvatica*

Figure 3.5. Identification guide for Eastern North American trees

It should be noted that the plants above can be planted with young American chestnuts in clearings in order to help provide nitrogen and biodiversity as the trees grow, but are not typically found in original American chestnut habitat in high numbers. In a more mature native oak/hickory/chestnut forest, one would expect to find plants that are more adapted to shaded conditions and high soil acidity. These would include high and low Bush blueberries, Mountain Laurel, Spicebush, Ghost pipe, Sassafras, Beech, Sweet Fern, Black Huckleberry, Spotted Wintergreen, Wood Fern, and many other native plants.

3.2 Fieldwork and Lab Work

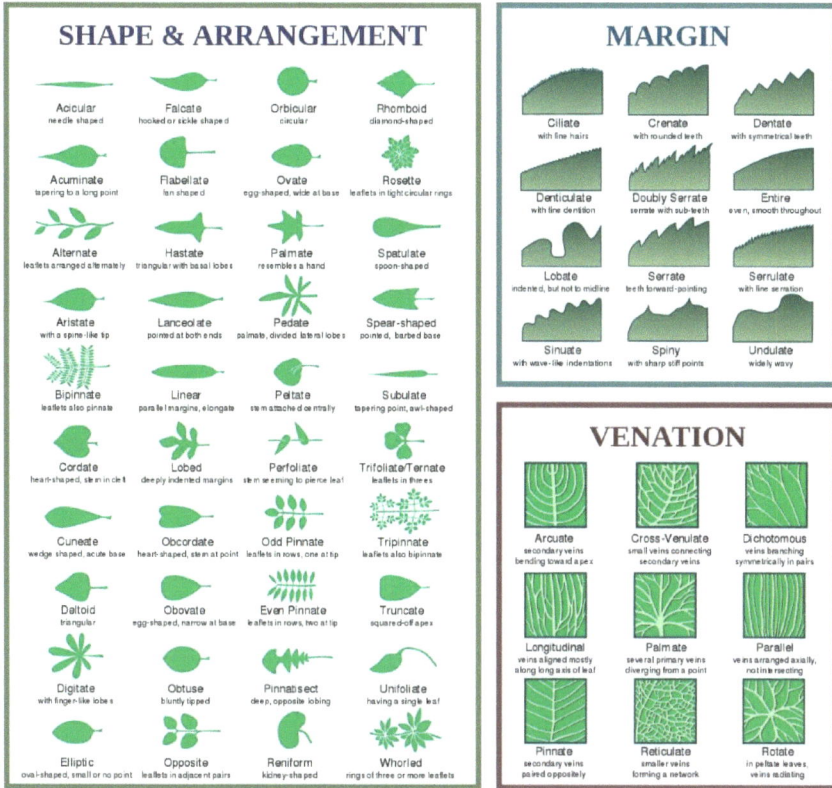

SHAPE & ARRANGEMENT

Acicular — needle shaped	Falcate — hooked or sickle shaped	Orbicular — circular	Rhomboid — diamond-shaped
Acuminate — tapering to a long point	Flabellate — fan shaped	Ovate — egg-shaped, wide at base	Rosette — leaflets in tight circular rings
Alternate — leaflets arranged alternately	Hastate — triangular with basal lobes	Palmate — resembles a hand	Spatulate — spoon-shaped
Aristate — with a spine-like tip	Lanceolate — pointed at both ends	Pedate — palmate, divided lateral lobes	Spear-shaped — pointed, barbed base
Bipinnate — leaflets also pinnate	Linear — parallel margins, elongate	Peltate — stem attached centrally	Subulate — tapering point, awl-shaped
Cordate — heart-shaped, stem in cleft	Lobed — deeply indented margins	Perfoliate — stem in seeming to pierce leaf	Trifoliate/Ternate — leaflets in threes
Cuneate — wedge shaped, acute base	Obcordate — heart-shaped, stem at point	Odd Pinnate — leaflets in rows, one at tip	Tripinnate — leaflets also bipinnate
Deltoid — triangular	Obovate — egg-shaped, narrow at base	Even Pinnate — leaflets in rows, two at tip	Truncate — squared-off apex
Digitate — with finger-like lobes	Obtuse — bluntly tipped	Pinnatisect — deep, opposite lobing	Unifoliate — having a single leaf
Elliptic — oval-shaped, small or no point	Opposite — leaflets in adjacent pairs	Reniform — kidney-shaped	Whorled — rings of three or more leaflets

MARGIN

Ciliate — with fine hairs	Crenate — with rounded teeth	Dentate — with symmetrical teeth
Denticulate — with fine dentition	Doubly Serrate — serrate with sub-teeth	Entire — even, smooth throughout
Lobate — indented, but not to midline	Serrate — teeth forward-pointing	Serrulate — with fine serration
Sinuate — with wave-like indentations	Spiny — with sharp stiff points	Undulate — widely wavy

VENATION

Arcuate — secondary veins bending toward apex	Cross-Venulate — small veins connecting secondary veins	Dichotomous — veins branching symmetrically in pairs
Longitudinal — veins aligned mostly along long axis of leaf	Palmate — several primary veins diverging from a point	Parallel — veins arranged axially, not intersecting
Pinnate — secondary veins paired oppositely	Reticulate — smaller veins forming a network	Rotate — in peltate leaves, veins radiating

Figure 3.6 Shape, arrangement, margin, venation types of leaves

In this part of the manual, we will learn how to collect plant specimens in the field. We will discuss how to dry, press and prepare plant specimens for analysis, as well as looking at key identifying features in the dissecting microscope.

3.2.1 Field specimen collection

Knowing and identifying forest tree species is an important task for examining biodiversity and forest ecology. In order to properly identify species that we are not familiar with, we collect leaf, flower and fruit specimens in the field. Above is a guide for some of the most common trees found in Eastern US shown in Figure 3.5.

In order to collect leaf specimens correctly, we need to understand leaf morphology. Leaves can be simple (one leaf blade) or compound (several leaflets on one stem). The leaf may be regular or irregular, smooth or with hair, bristles or spines. For example, hickory and ash have compound leaves, while chestnut, maple and birch have simple leaves. Figure 3.6 shows the common leaf shapes, arrangement, margins and venation, and their names. When collecting compound leaves, we have to make sure that we collect the entire leaf rather than separate leaflets. Based on Figure 3.6, we can classify the chestnut leaves as lanceolate in shape, with dentate margins and pinnate venation.

Next, we can use flowers to identify a species. Flowers are reproductive parts of a plant and the parts that will form a fruit. The stalk of a flower is called a pedicel, and sepals are the outer leaves located on the bottom of the flower (Figure 3.7). Flower petals are usually brightly colored to attract pollinators. Pollen is contained in the anther and the filament is a long tube that supports the anther, both forming a stamen. The pistil is where the pollen is deposited in the stigma, traveling through the style and fertilizing the ovary of the flower, for a fruit to grow.

Plants can have bisexual or unisexual flowers. Bisexual flowers have both, the pistil and the stamen in the same flower, while unisexual flowers will have only one. Plants that have unisex flowers will have a male and female plant and will need both in proximity and wind or pollinators to achieve fertilization. Bisexual flowers can self-pollinate or can be self-incompatible. Self-incompatible flowers need proximity of other plants and wind or a pollinator to achieve fertilization. American chestnut flowers are unisex catkins. See figure 3.8 for example of flower types.

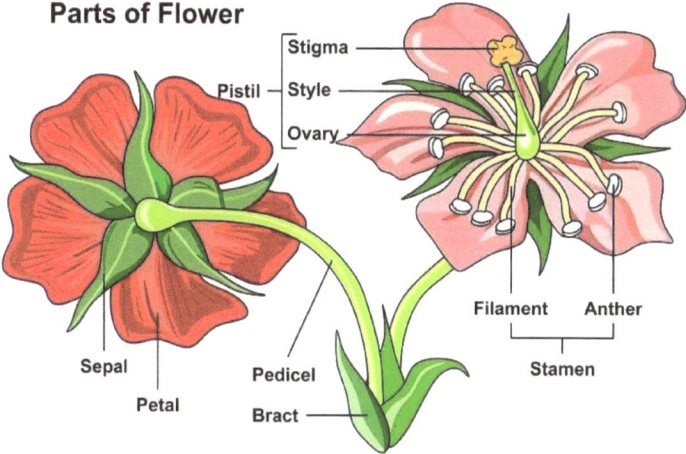

Figure 3.7 Parts of the flower

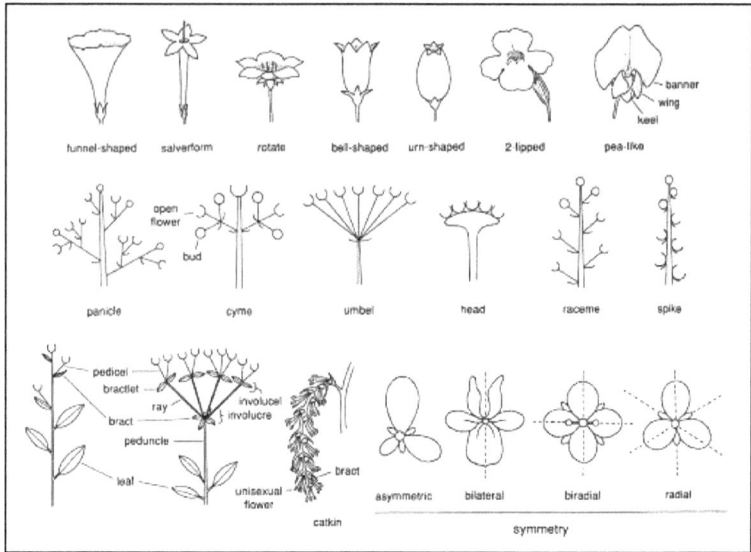

Figure 3.8 Flower types

3.2.2 Preparing and looking at specimens in the lab

In order to properly collect the leaf specimens, choose leaves that are representative of the average size of leaves on a tree. Look for specimens without tears, fungus, insect or any other damage. Pick leaves directly from the tree rather than from the ground. Lay the leaves flat between layers of paper, then add cardboard on top, and secure between two flat boards with tightening screws of the leaf press.

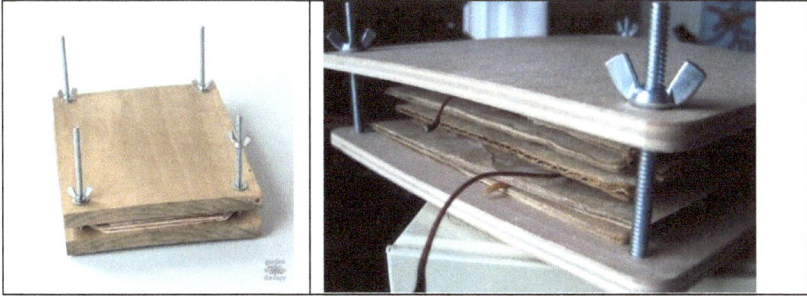

Figure 3.9 Leaf press

The leaf press is something that can be made at home by drilling 4 holes at the corners of 2 boards for tightening screws to go through them (see Figure 3.9). Specimens should be left to dry undisturbed for several weeks. The exact time will depend on size, moisture content of the leaf and of the airflow of the space where the specimens are kept. Keep them out of direct sunlight to avoid fading and out of moisture to avoid mold.

When the specimens are ready, they can be analyzed under a dissecting microscope. A dissecting microscope has a larger working distance between the specimen plate and the lens, which differs from a compound microscope's smaller working distance. Another difference is the dissecting microscope has a lower magnification than a compound microscope (used for microbiology). The light shines down on the specimen as opposed to shining up through it, which means we can examine the surface characteristics without having to prepare and stain a slide of the specimen. A dissecting microscope (Figure 3.10) is helpful in identifying specific features of plant leaves that can help distinguishing between species. For example, leaf hairs may not be visible with a naked eye, but observing the presence with a microscope, can help us to distinguish between different chestnut species.

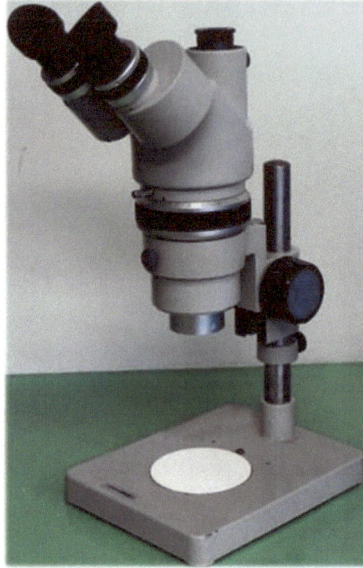

Figure 3.11 Dissecting microscope

4.1 American Chestnut Propagation and Reforestation

In this part of the manual, we will discuss hands-on aspects of propagating, planting and taking care of the American chestnut trees. The information below will be of interest to anyone who wants to start a reforestation program with chestnut trees, or someone why would like to plant a few American chestnut trees on their property. It's important to properly propagate and plant chestnut in the best suited environment to ensure its successful establishment due to the difficulties it faces in the wild as a result of the chestnut blight.

4.1.1 Suitable ecological conditions for the propagation of the American chestnut

American chestnut trees are late successional species that are shade-tolerant and grow well under a canopy of other forest trees. The chestnut trees grow best in the upland deciduous forest with oaks, red maple, sugar maple, and beech. However, when planted as 1-year old seedlings, the trees will benefit from and tolerate direct sun, so long as they have adequate moisture. Seedlings transplanted in direct sun at 1-year of age will reach maturity and start producing nuts quicker than in the shade. Getting established quicker also helps the trees to escape predation by deer. As a result, it's best to plant them in areas that get at least 6 hours of sun a day and have an open canopy for quick establishment and growth of the seedlings. The chestnuts like well-drained, sandy and rocky soils that are fertile and with a slightly acidic pH. The seedlings and the trees will not do well in clay soils that collect standing water.

American chestnuts flourish in soil conditions rich in fungal organisms and conducive of **mycorrhizae-forming potentials**. The mycorrhizae are mutualistic associations between plant roots and fungal organisms that help the plant with mineral uptake as well as with water absorption. In exchange, the plant (such as the chestnut) provides carbohydrates to the fungus that it produces through photosynthesis. Optimally, the American chestnut should be planted in soils that are rich in fungal elements, such as the forest soils. When planting chestnuts in open grassy fields, a fungal application to the roots could be beneficial to introduce mycorrhizae.

4.2 Fieldwork

This part of the manual goes into detail about the practical and logistical aspects of seed propagation, site selection, seedling transplanting, short-term and long-term maintenance of American chestnuts.

4.2.1 Chestnut propagation and site selection

Since we now know how to identify American chestnut trees, we can try and find them in the wild in the hopes of collecting the seeds. However, that may be a difficult task as we also learned that most chestnuts were eradicated due to the chestnut blight. The few that remain very rarely reach maturity to reproduce. In case you are lucky enough to find an American chestnut tree that produces nuts, the best time to collect them would be in early fall. American chestnut burrs start developing in June and are mature by September or October. Collect seeds from under the tree that shows no signs of damage by wildlife, insects or pathogens. You may see that burrs start to split open, which is a sign of seed maturity. Make sure that the seeds collected are viable. Choose seeds that look healthy, plump and firm, without any signs of fungus, mold, and rot or softening. Chestnut tree needs to be cross-pollinated, which means it needs to be in proximity of other American chestnut trees mature enough to flower. If cross-pollination did not occur, the tree may still produce nuts, but they will be small and shriveled.

Chestnuts should first be stored in a cold environment before they are ready to germinate. It's best to put them in a plastic bag with slightly damp peat moss and poke holes for ventilation, and store in the refrigerator at 32 F to 35 F for 3 months. After that, seeds can be started in January or February indoors to prevent rodent predation. American chestnuts are highly desired by rodents that can sniff them out from far away and will dig the seeds out from under ground. Seeds should be started in long plastic containers that are at least 10 to15 inches long as shown in Figure 4.1.

Figure 4.1 Chestnut seedlings in long plastic containers.

If you can't find plastic potting containers shown in Figure 4.1, you can use a milk carton. It's best to cut off the bottom and cover it with mesh to allow air to circulate and for water to drain. Chestnut seedlings like well-drained but fertile soil. As such, most potting mixes will likely be too dense. It's best to mix 1 part sand, 1 part mulch and 1 part peat moss as a potting mix for propagating chestnuts, and moisten it before planting. Sow the chestnuts sideways 1 to 1.5 inches deep. Keep the seeds in the sunny spot, keep them moist but do not over water. The seeds should start germinating by early spring. In early May, the seedlings can be transferred outside to get the full benefit of the summer sun, though if they dry out too quickly they can be placed in partial shade. It is important to keep them safe from rodents at this time. You can do so by putting chicken wire all around and on top of them creating a cage. Let the surface of the soil dry out between waterings. By late summer, you can start preparing the seedlings for transplanting by gradually giving them less water for about a month prior to transplanting.

If seeds are not available, there are several places and farms that can sell American chestnut seedlings:

American Chestnut Council. Cadillac, MI

Chief River Nursery. Grafton, WI

Go Native Tree Farm. Manheim, PA

Planting should occur in the fall for best establishment as the tree focuses on root growth in the fall and winter rather than on growing leaves and flowers that take up a lot of tree's energy. The trees can be planted in late fall, ideally before the ground freezes. Choose the seedlings that look the strongest after the hardening off process. If the aim is to get at least 2 mature trees so that fertilization can occur, then we need to plant at least 4 to 6 seedlings to account for mortality. Now we need to decide where and how close to plant. Plant seedlings at least 10 to 20 feet apart as they will grow large. Choose a spot that lets 6 hours or more of sunlight for best initial growth. This will also encourage early establishment. However, chestnuts are shade-tolerant and will grow, although slower, in partial shade. As mentioned before, American chestnuts like fertile, well drained, slightly acidic soils (pH 4.5-5.6). Once you have the site, you can test the soil pH using pH strips. To do so, dig up a handful of top soil, mix with distilled water until runny, dip pH strip for 10-20 seconds (or per package instructions) and read the pH. If the pH is neutral or basic, planting can still occur after the pH is adjusted. This can be done using various products available at garden centers which include Aluminum Sulfate.

4.2.2 Planting and Initial care

Planting. Start by digging a 2 feet deep by 1.5 feet wide hole to encourage aeration and drainage. If soils are rocky, it's best to remove large rocks that can disturb root growth. Small rocks will not hinder root development. Chestnuts should not be planted in clay soils. If the site is an open field such as grassland, then a mycorrhizae inoculation containing the Pigskin Puffball (*Scleroderma citrinum*) could be beneficial. If planted in the forest or recently logged forest, the soil may contain sufficient mycorrhizae. Take care to take out the seedling from the container without disturbing the roots. Apply mycorrhizae to the roots, then place in the middle of the hole suspended while covering with dirt, mulch and sand (if needed). The new tree should be positioned so that the entire trunk is above ground and only the roots in the soil. It is necessary to compact the soil underneath the new tree so that it does not sink in the planting hole. Roots should be spread out to grow away from the trunk. Gently press soil down into the home around the roots to remove any air pockets. Be sure to water thoroughly after planting.

Plan to inspect the trees once every 3 months for pest and pathogen control, weed control, soil pH testing, applying fertilizer and pruning.

The trees will need about an inch of water a week during the summer of their first season. If it has not rained, plan to water once a week. The new tree should be positioned so that the entire trunk is above ground and only the roots in the soil. It is necessary to compact the soil underneath the new tree so that it does not sink in the planting hole. Roots should be spread out to grow away from the trunk.

Pest control. In eastern North America, the most common setback in chestnut growing is browse by deer. Seedlings are also predated by rodents. In order to protect the new seedlings in the wild, we can apply a rodent and a deer guard. Figure 4.2 shows ready to transplant seedlings on the left, a rodent guard in the middle, and a deer guard on the right. We can use tall plastic tree tubes or chicken/garden wire fencing in combination with fine mesh wire rodent guards and supportive staking, as they render superior protection for deer and other mammalian predators. The tubes also act as mini-greenhouses around the trees, promoting faster growth. Make sure to stick the wire at least one inch under the soil around the roots to prevent rodents from being able to access the seeds. Inspect the protective tree tubes regularly for damage and to make sure they stay straight. As the trees grow, they may need to be tucked back into their tubes at times.

Figure 4.2 Chestnut seedlings ready to be transplanted. Transplanted seeding with a rodent guard. Transplanted seedling with a deer guard.

Soil pH and fertilizer. Soil pH should be tested and adjusted every year (if needed) until the desired level is reached. The adjustments can be done via applying Sulphur-containing fertilizers such us Epsoma organic Holy Tone. Once the optimal level is reached, the test can be performed every other year. There are several considerations that go into selecting the proper regime for the trees and applying fertilizing products to help maintain the planting. Fertilizers provide an added boost in the trees' early years, but are not necessary for the trees' survival. It would be best long-term for the trees to rely on the companion plants and environment that allows for sequestration of needed nutrients and nitrogen. When fertilizers are to be used, utilize organic fertilizers paying attention to all labels. Products such as fish emulsion fertilizers, and granular slow-release organic products by Espoma such as Tree Tone meet organic fertilizer standards. Fertilizers should be applied in early spring only, and not the first year. Fertilizers should be spread evenly around the drip-zone of the trees, or an 18" circle if the tree has not branched yet.

Watering. Watering will be required at planting and if there is prolonged dry weather during the first spring and summer after planting. The trees will need about an inch of water a week during the spring and summer of their first season. If it has not rained, plan to water once a week. American chestnut trees quickly develop a very deep taproot and should not need to be watered once established.

Pruning. Appropriate pruning protocols will keep American chestnut trees healthier, create a more attractive appearance and increase nut production. Of highest priority is to remove any branches that might cause the tree problems in the future. This includes dead branches, broken branches, and branches affected by blight.

The following standards should be used:

- American chestnut tree pruning should typically take place in dry weather in late July.
- However, pruning back a broken or diseased branch can be done at other times to optimize the tree's health so long as the weather is dry. That said, pruning should NEVER happen in springtime when blight is most active (releasing spores). Even a diseased branch should not be pruned then because spores can go right into the wound into the healthy wood that was just exposed.
- Use clean sharp secateurs or a sharp saw to reduce possibility of infection.
- Ensure tree is growing straight up through protective tube. Occasionally they may fall out the slit and become exposed to

deer browse. The central leader system is to be used. In this system, all leaders but the strongest are removed to encourage tree height.

- When pruning, trim off side branches from the main leader on each tree until it reaches a height taller than the tube. Cut flush to trunk without damaging branch collar.
- Do not remove more than 1/3 of the chestnut tree in any one year.
- Pruning can be less frequent when trees reach their tube height. The objective behind training and pruning young trees will help to develop a strong tree framework, prevent many serious problems before they develop, and support nut production.
- Ensure name tag is visible at each tree or that name is legible on the tree tube.
- Cut back (coppice) any companion trees/shrubs that have grown to block light from the Chestnuts. Cut back to the ground any existing saplings or shrubs that are encroaching on the Chestnuts.

Weeding. Planting American chestnut trees along with native beneficial nitrogen-fixing and nutrient-accumulating plants contributes greatly to the trees' health and growth as well as to the local biodiversity.

Follow the following weeding standards:

- Manual weeding of competing or invasive plants or grasses within 3 feet of base of trees. This zone may be expanded as the trees grow. Take care not to remove or harm

- companion plants (see Figure 3.4 from the previous chapter for the list of companion species).
- Periodic mulching
- Application of organic herbicide (only if necessary).

4.2.3 Long-term care

Long-term maintenance considerations include pathogen and blight control, deer protection and replanting

Pathogens and Blight Control We expect that any planting sites within the North-Eastern US will eventually be attacked by natural infections of the blight. Other pathogen attacks (such as *Phytophthora cinnamomi*) may be possible although to date, none have been reported in New Jersey and Pennsylvania areas. That said, as with insect attacks, vigilance to sudden changes in survival or health of the trees is expected during all inspection visits. Blight will appear as a reddish brown scar on the bark of the tree and will spread to go around the trunk or the branch (see figure 4.3 for an example.)

With respect to addressing the blight occurrence, the following standards are to be followed:

- If there are any signs of blight, remove any dead branches to the nearest branch collar.
- Remove blighted branches by cutting back to the nearest uninfected branch collar. This is preferred during dry summer weather or during winter.
- If blight affects the trunk of any tree, a decision must be made whether to apply a "mud-pack" dressing which may prolong the lifespan of a tree, cut, or remove the tree. The decision will depend on severity of infection and hardiness of the tree.

Figure 4.3 Sighting of blight on a trunk of an American chestnut tree

Deer and Pest Control. Once the trees have matured and grown several feet above the level of the tree tubes, the tubes will be removed and replaced with 3-4 foot tall cylinders of chicken wire garden fencing to deter deer from rubbing the bark with antlers. The rodent guards can be removed sooner, after the second season.

Replanting. The overall goal is to ensure that as many trees that have partial or full resistance to the blight make it to maturity, and to preserve the genetics of the species. However, any trees that do not survive should be replanted, unless the decision is made to leave the space for adjacent trees if necessary.

GLOSSARY

Alpha Diversity - measures biodiversity on small scale at a habitat unit, for example, a forest patch, and refers to species richness, focusing on identifying the number of different species in a small area.

Beta Diversity – measures biodiversity between 2 habitats, for example an old growth forest patch and a young recruiting forest. Beta diversity is also diversity that is measured along a gradient such as forest species change going along an elevation gradient. Beta diversity is used to compare how an ecosystem changes going up the slope.

Biodiversity is the variety of plant and animal life on the planet or in a specific area. Biodiversity is also interchangeable with terms like species diversity or species richness.

Chestnut Blight - Cryphonectria parasitica, a parasitic fungus of chestnut trees. Naturally found in South East Asia, accidental introductions led to invasive populations of C. parasitica in North America and Europe.

Core-Borer – a tool to extract a section of wood tissue from a living tree with relatively minor injury to the plant itself.

Cross-Pollination – a type of pollination when one plant pollinates a plant of another species. The two plants' genetic material combines and the resulting seeds from the pollination will have characteristics of both varieties and is a new variety.

Diameter at Breast Height (DBH) – the standard of measuring trees. DBH refers to the tree diameter measured at 4.5 feet above the ground. DBG can be measured quickly with a specialty calibrated diameter tape, often referred to as a d-tape, that displays the diameter measurement when wrapped around the circumference of a tree.

Dissecting Microscope – also known as stereo or stereoscopic microscope. It is an optical microscope that is designed for low magnification observation of a specimen.

Early Successional Tree Species - fast-growing and sun-loving trees that quickly create vegetative cover on degraded land and do not require fertile soils. Usually, their leaves, bark or roots have antibacterial or anti-fungal properties that deter pathogens, and this is used medicinally in many traditional cultures.

Forest Disturbance - an external event that causes partial or complete destruction of forest biomass. While these events are often seen as catastrophic in nature, they are actually an integral part of a forest ecosystem. In fact, forests and their species are usually adapted to the type of disturbance that is most common in the area, and these disturbances dictate forest regeneration strategy and 'successional dynamics.'

Forest Disturbance, Human – also called Anthropogenic, and includes climate change, pollution, logging, clearcutting, and the introduction of invasive species and pathogens.

Forest Disturbance, Natural – examples include fires, landslides resulting from heavy rains or floods, wind, tornadoes, hurricanes and typhoons, volcanic eruptions, earthquakes, natural pathogens, and natural animal grazing.

Forest Strata – scientists divide forests into different strata or layers for easy reference. Each of the layers represents a different environment and supports different life forms.

Gamma diversity - measures biodiversity within a landscape or a region. The gamma diversity also measures a rate at which new species are added to a landscape.

Hygrometer - an instrument used for measuring the amount of humidity in the air.

Ink Disease - Phytophthora cinnamomi is a soil-borne water mould that produces an infection which causes a condition in plants variously called "root rot" or "dieback" or in certain Castanea species "ink disease." The plan pathogen is one of the world's most invasive species and is present in over 70 countries around the world.

Keystone Species – species that provide food and shelter for many animal and plant species and define the ecosystem.

Late Successional Species - slow growing, shade-needing trees that colonize well established forest patches and lead to climax forest.

Leaf Morphology - a study of external form and structure of leaves.

Lixiviation – separation of soluble from insoluble material by use of an appropriate solvent, and drawing off the solution.

Mycorrhizae-Forming Potentials - mutualistic associations between plant roots and fungal organisms that help the plant with mineral uptake as well as with water absorption.

Mycorrhizae Inoculation – a technique to amend soil or plant' roots with mycorrhizal fungi, to stimulate root growth, increase the absorptive root area by sending long hyphal strands into the soil, and from a protective barrier or mantle around fine roots.

Mid Successional Species – trees that are secondary colonizers and require semi-shade to thrive and invade areas that have already been colonized by early successional species. These trees have slower growth and are longer-living than early successional species.

Pedology – a discipline within soil science which focuses on understanding and characterizing soil formation, evolution, and the theoretical frameworks through which a soil body is understood, often in the context of the natural environment.

Simpson's Diversity Index - a measure of diversity which takes into account the number of species present, as well as the relative abundance of each species. As species richness and evenness increase, so diversity increases.

Stand Replacement – a high-intensity event like a fire that kills most or all of the trees in the stand.

Successional Dynamics - stages of forest growth and maturity.

Successional Tree Species - colonizing species that grow in a cleared area or smaller gap formed after a disturbance of the original species over a set period of time.

Transect Line – a straight line going through the study area along with the data to be collected, usually recording different animal or plant species present. A transect could be anywhere from 25 meters (75 feet) to 100 meters (300 feet) long, depend on the study area.

Understory Tree – trees and shrubs growing between the forest canopy and the forest floor. Plants in the understory comprise an assortment of seedlings and saplings of canopy trees together with specialist understory shrubs and herbs.

INDEX

floodplain, 4
Florida chinquapin, 46
forest age, 1, 7, 10
forest cover, 38
forest disturbance, 1, 3,
    10, 71
forest extraction, 6
forest management,
    10, 77
forest patch, 6, 8-10,
    14, 16-17, 24, 26
forest transect, 1, 17
fragmentation, 6, 26
Fraxinus americana, 50
Fraxinus nigra, 50
frugivore, 24
functionally extinct, 42

G

Gamma diversity, 27,
    72
Growth Factor, 18-19

H

Hygrometer, 23, 72

I

Ink Disease, 43, 72

K

keystone, 5, 44, 72

L

**Late Successional
    Species**, 8, 18, 58
Leaf Morphology, 53,
    72
Lixiviation, 22, 72

M

Mycorrhizae, 59, 63,
    72-73

P

Pathogen, 3, 5-7, 14,
    16, 43, 60, 63, 68,
    71-72
Pedology, 22, 73
*Phytophthora
    cinnamomi*, 43, 68,
    72
Pigskin Puffball, 63
Pin Oak, 19
pinnate venation, 53
Pinus strobus, 30, 50
Platanus occidentalis,
    14, 30
plot area, 37, 39
potassium, 22, 48
Propagation, 58, 60
purple prairie clover,
    48-49

Q

Quercus alba, 30, 50

R

Red Maple, 4, 7-8, 19,
    30, 40, 45, 50, 58
Red Oak, 8, 19, 50
Redbud, 19, 49
River Birch, 4, 19
Robinia pseudoacacia,
    14, 49
rodent guard, 64-65, 69

S

Sassafras, 50, 51
Stand Replacement, 3,
    5, 73
Strata, 10, 16, 31
Successional Dynamics,
    2, 71, 73
Sycamore, 14, 30, 40

T

Transect, 2, 16, 17, 31
Tree Identification, 1,
    21

U

Understory Tree, 10,
    74

W

White oak, 19, 30, 40,
    50

CONTRIBUTORS' BIOGRAPHIES

Mariya Chechina – Mariya is the lead contributor of the Manual. Her PhD focused on social and ecological suitability of over 100 tree species to be used for reforestation in the Philippines (published in Ecosphere). There, she also examined the effectiveness of land-use policies (published in Conservation and Society Journal) and developed a forest management plan to reduce illegal logging and expand livelihoods. She worked on Antinanco's American chestnut program since 2019, developing the Northeastern ecosystems' restoration manual for high schools and colleges.

Tom Shotzbarger – Tom is a practitioner, educator, author, consultant, conference speaker and industry representative with more than 45 years in the Green Industry and numerous certifications in Arboriculture, Horticulture and Turfgrass Management. He is the Grounds Manager for Graver Arboretum of Muhlenberg College, PA, and is involved in the American Chestnut Tree Conservation project with the intention of helping others expand their knowledge to act on improving our woodlands. Tom is presently focused on learning more about watershed management, wildlife habitat conservation and, of course, planting American chestnut trees.

Joseph A. Resch - Joseph has had a deep relationship with plants since beginning to care for them at the age of five, and over a decade of experience in the nursery and landscape trade. His lifelong love for the forest and wildlife inspired him to become the project leader of Antinanco's program to help bring back the American Chestnut tree, knowing the immense value that this tree once had. Joe enjoys leading hands-on planting and tree care workshops for youth and adults. His goal is to help restore the forests of the East Coast back to their previous fruitfulness while inspiring future generations to become responsible stewards of the Land.

Yannick Neveux - first assessed policies and private support to conservation in France. For his MSc in Canada, he studied the impacts of climate change and roads on North America's vegetation, ungulates and land-use. He identified potential reserves that maintain intactness and connectivity for self-sustenance. As TropicForest cofounder, he worked with Mariya Chechina in the Philippines setting-up a nursery and a 4 ha plantation to test the growth of 22 native trees. He enjoyed helping Antinantco with planting a few hundred Chestnut trees in New-jersey and Pennsylvania.

Olga Sher - Olga was born in the Volga-Ural region of Russia. From an early age, she was interested in herbal studies, traditional healing modalities, medicinal plants and mushrooms. Presently, Olga's home is in Holmdel, NJ, where she raises two children, practices law, and advocates for the preservation of earth-based ways and indigenous traditions through organizing community service projects, workshops and classes with Antinanco Earth Arts School. Olga has been involved with the American Chestnut Revival project since its inception in 2018.

Mark A. Klingler – Mark is an award-winning artist residing in the Pocono Mountains of eastern PA. Formerly a scientific illustrator at Carnegie Museum of Natural History in Pittsburgh, PA, Klingler collaborated with scientists for more than 30 years to visually interpret the stories of newly discovered species as well as extinct creatures from the past. Klingler is a recipient of the Society for Vertebrate Paleontology's Lanzendorf art prize and has illustrated popular science books such as Field Guide to the Natural World of New York City and Hunt for the Dawn Monkey.

www.ingramcontent.com/pod-product-compliance
Lightning Source LLC
Chambersburg PA
CBHW041225280326
41928CB00045B/65